ROWvotions
Volume VIII

✦

The Devotional Book of Rivers of the World

Ben Mathes with Karin M. Clack

iUniverse, Inc.
New York Bloomington

ROWvotions Volume VIII
The Devotional Book of Rivers of the World

iUniverse books may be ordered through booksellers or by contacting:

iUniverse
1663 Liberty Drive
Bloomington, IN 47403
www.iuniverse.com
1-800-Authors (1-800-288-4677)

Because of the dynamic nature of the Internet, any Web addresses or links contained in this book may have changed since publication and may no longer be valid. The views expressed in this work are solely those of the author and do not necessarily reflect the views of the publisher, and the publisher hereby disclaims any responsibility for them.

ISBN: 978-1-4401-3627-6 (sc)
ISBN: 978-1-4401-3628-3 (ebook)

Printed in the United States of America

iUniverse rev. date: 4/1/2009

Contents

Foreword

Since 1978, Dr. Ben Mathes has been traveling the world on behalf of our Lord. His ministry has taken him to over 50 countries. Currently the president of Rivers of the World (ROW), Dr. Mathes helps to provide people, money, and other items to reach the world's poorest with a ministry of compassion and hope.

When in the States, Dr. Mathes speaks in almost 200 cities a year. His radio ministry reaches over three million listeners in 48 states.

These devotions are based on his radio ministry.

To contact ROW and Dr. Mathes:

www.row.org

Dr. Ben C. Mathes
PMB 64
6625 Hwy. 53 East, Suite 410
Dawsonville, Ga. 30534

706-344-1283

Ben@row.org

Preface

The very hand of God orchestrated this book of devotions, along with the previous volumes. The opportunity to write these devotions is an answer to several years of prayer in which I asked the Lord for an open door to write solely for Him. I have desired for some time to use the gift of writing He has blessed me with so that I may bless others in the furtherance of His kingdom.

Early in 2006, while living in Oregon, I had heard several radio spots featuring Rivers of the World (ROW) on a contemporary Christian radio station. One evening after I browsed the ROW web site I decided to send an e-mail volunteering my services to the organization for proofreading or editing materials.

Within a few days, ROW President Ben Mathes replied to my e-mail noting it was an answer to their prayers as they were looking for someone to take their radio spots and create articles for future publications. I immediately saw God's hand in the midst of this awesome opportunity.

I gathered some of my previous published articles, e-mailed them as samples of my work and within a day my journey as a freelance "ghost" writer had begun.

These devotions have given me a chance to allow the Holy Spirit to inspire me and to let His words flow through me. I hope the devotions will touch the hearts and lives of people in need of the Savior or those who simply desire a closer walk with Jesus.

Much prayer takes place before words are placed on a page. These prayers include asking Him to give to me the right words to make an impact upon others and for Him to guide me to the specific Scripture He would have me to incorporate in each devotion.

I humbly thank my Lord for His daily presence in my life and for allowing me to be His instrument to reach a lost and dying world for Him. If but one soul accepts salvation because of these devotions, then I have fulfilled my mission.

There is another spirit that nudges me to take my thoughts and carefully and creatively arrange them on paper so that others may be inspired and blessed. Her name is Anna W. King, my dear grandmother whose written words were silenced in the fall of 1997 as her Lord called her home. She still gives me inspiration and I hope I can continue to "speak" for her until my Lord calls me home.

To God be the glory.

Karin M. Clack
Colorado Springs, CO

Acknowledgments

I am so grateful that the Lord has enabled me to experience so many things in so many places! Christian missions are exciting to say the least! My heartfelt thanks and prayers go to my wife, Dr. Mickie Mathes, for her courage; to "3," for running Rivers of the World (ROW) with a gentle spirit; to Liz Snodgrass, our graphic designer, for capturing the essence of ROW in her work; to Karin Clack, whose writing skills shine in each devotion; to Winston, my dog, whose memory lives on; and to all who make ROW possible. God bless you!

Ben C. Mathes
Dawsonville, Ga.

Art of Contentment

Do you realize that you can be at home anywhere in the world? As I prepare for a trip to Prague to visit my wife, Dr. Mickie Mathes, I recall a car commercial that I once saw on television. The black and white commercial featured a man dressed in a trench coat. He walks across that famous bridge in Prague and he is talking about an automobile, but viewers never actually see the automobile.

I am going to get a trench coat and walk across that bridge in Prague while I visit my wife, who will be taking five days off from her duties at the University of Qatar in the Middle East, where she is a Fulbright Scholar. I can tell you this for a fact, that wherever Mickie is, that is home. Whether we are actually in our home in Georgia, at her temporary home in the Middle East or spending five days together in Prague, it is home to me because home is wherever you find your heart and the people whom you love.

Paul discovered the true secret to contentment and being at home wherever he was at any particular moment in his life. We read in Philippians 4:12-13:

"I know what it is to be in need, and I know what it is to have plenty. I have learned the secret of being content in any and every situation, whether well fed or hungry, whether living in plenty or in want. I can do everything through him who gives me strength."

We can find peace, joy and contentment in every situation in our lives no matter if the situation is joyous or devastating because it is through Christ, and Christ alone, that we find our strength. If you are experiencing a particularly difficult time in your life let me encourage you to change your perspective. Instead of focusing upon the problem, praise the God who is greater than all your problems.

Captivating

Most of the time, I simply drive right on by and don't pay any attention. Sometimes, though, when my eyes see them they make me laugh, are very poignant and make me think. But, I usually don't notice them. You are probably wondering what I am talking about—billboards.

I don't normally notice those signs that are strategically placed along highways. The only time I notice billboards is if they really catch my attention—like recently. Two billboards in particular caught my attention. The first sign was straightforward and simple with only one word on it—quit. Let me say that again—the sign said quit.

That one word is so very powerful. It means if you are living your life in an unhealthy manner, then quit because it is likely killing you. If you find yourself being abusive toward someone, then stop because it is killing somebody else—physically and emotionally. It is just like when we accept salvation. We soon discover that our love for the Lord becomes greater than our desire to sin and thus we quit, relinquish or repent so that we can grow in the likeness of Him.

The other billboard that caught my attention said, "Your wife knows." Now that is scary! The second part of the sign said that such and such insurance company is the best. I can assure you that your wife knows that you are the best thing that has ever happened to her. I will go a step further and say that you probably have realized through the years that your wife is the most remarkable thing that has taken place in your life.

We discover towards the end of Proverbs 31 that the woman described was an asset to her husband. She did more than the usual household tasks. She was a gifted seamstress and cook, she was wise in business dealings, she was careful to keep supplies on hand at all times and she not only provided for her family, but also for those in need. She was never idle, but always busy working and serving others.

We read in Proverbs 31:10-11:

"A wife of noble character who can find? She is worth far more than rubies. Her husband has full confidence in her and lacks nothing of value."

It would be difficult for a man who found a wife such as this to not be captivated by her. Let us remember today that we have captured the heart of One who is greater than our spouse—the Lord Jesus Christ.

Visit the Rivers of the World (ROW) web site at www.row.org today to see how you and your spouse can deepen your relationship by volunteering your time.

Consider Others

No one really noticed Lolita because she was just the housekeeper. Oh, the family was grateful for Lolita, but they never really paid much attention to this dear woman. That was until the family was pinned down in the middle of a battle during a horrible civil war.

Things began to get desperate after the family had eaten all of their food and drank all their water. In the midst of this crisis, Lolita disappeared. The family was outraged—how dare she leave them during this situation. The family's outrage soon turned to joy and gratitude when Lolita returned with food, water and supplies that ultimately sustained the family through this difficult time. Never again did the family take Lolita for granted.

Pause for a moment and reflect upon those people in your life whom you normally just pass by without acknowledging or even noticing. Go out of your way today to stop what you are doing and demonstrate to these people that you care for them and are grateful for all they do. These people may include your babysitter, the teenager who bags your groceries, the mail carrier who delivers mail in your neighborhood regardless of the weather or the person who mows your grass when the temperatures are sweltering in the summertime.

Allow me to take this opportunity on behalf of Rivers of the World (ROW) to say thank you to our radio listeners, to those folks who visit our web site, to people who generously give in support of this ministry and the many people who lift ROW up in prayer each day.

In everything that we do, we must remember to consider others before ourselves. We are instructed in Philippians 2:3-4:

"Do nothing out of selfish ambition or vain conceit, but in humility consider others better than yourselves. Each of you should look not only to your own interests, but also to the interests of others."

Entrust All to Him

Today is Dec. 17, 2008. There is no need to adjust your watch or change your calendar. I know it is only February, but, today, we are going to look back over the year 2008. We are going to examine all of the things that we accomplished and all those things that we left undone.

Now I know that you, and so many people, made all sorts of promises to yourself in January. You promised to cut back on eating sweets, to exercise 30 minutes each day, to lose all those extra pounds you gained over the holidays and to eat more vegetables. You may have even made some serious spiritual promises, such as to begin tithing, to go to church more, to read the Bible more and to spend more time with the Lord.

As the year ended, I wonder what happened to all those promises you made. They vanished as quickly as the passing of the year. Now I know we may slip up and eat a piece of chocolate, get too tired to go for that walk and get too distracted to read the Bible. I even know that some of our sins catch up with us from time to time.

Let me encourage you before it is too late, to start each day examining what you were able to accomplish last month, last week and yesterday. Are there some things that you keep putting off and some things that you know you need to be doing each day? Where do you hope to be at the end of this year in your career, in your marriage and in your relationship with Christ? I don't know what all this year holds for me but I do know I'll be spending time in a jungle somewhere.

Sometimes I believe we forget that we must entrust everything that we have and all that we hope to be, unto Christ. We read in Proverbs 16:3:

"Commit to the LORD whatever you do, and your plans will succeed."

It is quite simple. You want to lose that weight, then pray and ask the

Lord for discipline. You want to be healthier, then pray and ask the Lord for wisdom. You want a better marriage, then pray and ask the Lord how you can be a better person for your spouse. Everything large, small, major, minor and everything in between must be committed unto Christ in order for us to be successful.

Eternal Perspective

People often ask me how I manage to travel to so many countries and cities every year and keep my wits about myself. On average, I visit about 200 cities a year and I am in a different country every month. How do I manage all this traveling, you might ask. My secret is wherever I am I consider myself to be home. Whenever I get off a plane and whenever I get out of a car the first thing I say is, "I'm home!" and then I don't feel like I need to be somewhere else.

Through all of my travels my heart goes with me allowing me to care for the people Rivers of the World (ROW) serves and enabling me to leave a part of myself behind. I may not always know where I am, but I know that I am there with all of my heart and I am at home.

Every day is Valentine's Day when you serve the Lord. Today, let me encourage you to take a piece of your heart and share it with somebody else.

Whether you are a frequent flyer or one who stays close to home, it is important for you to adopt an eternal perspective. During times when we are away from the comforts of home traveling on business or vacation and even during those times we are away from home confined in a hospital, we can still feel at home and at peace in the Lord. They key is to put into practice Colossians 3:2, which says:

"Set your minds on things above, not on earthly things."

Faith in Action

Rivers of the World (ROW) has been presented with an opportunity that comes only once in a lifetime. I am coming to you from the country of Qatar in the Middle East. ROW has been granted permission to help build a Christian church complex in Doha, the capital of Qatar.

The Emir of Qatar, His Highness Sheikh Hamad bin Khalifa Al Thani, has offered land on which to build the country's first Christian churches since the seventh century when Islam took root in the Gulf country. The "church city" site will contain five church complexes—The Church of the Epiphany, Roman Catholic, Byzantine Orthodox, Oriental Orthodox and Indian Churches.

The Anglican Centre will be constructed on a site provided by the State of Qatar. The Centre will provide a welcome for all Anglican, Protestant and Evangelical Christians to address both their spiritual and community needs. At the heart of the Centre will be the Church of the Epiphany.

The Centre will be built in a series of stages. The first stage is estimated to cost 1.5 million Qatar Riyals, or $3 million U.S. dollars. The detailed design is in progress and the groundbreaking is scheduled for May 2008. ROW has decided to partner in this project because we think our readers and listeners might appreciate having the opportunity to be a part of something unique, unprecedented, and remarkable: that of building a Christian church in a Muslim country.

It is easy to call yourself a Christian but the true measure of a person who is genuinely following Christ is one whose faith is put into action. We are reminded in James 2:26 (NKJV):

"For as the body without the spirit is dead, so faith without works is dead also."

11

Prayerfully consider using a portion of the financial resources the Lord has blessed you with to assist with the construction of this church complex. This will speak volumes to those living in the Muslim country of Qatar of the importance of your faith.

To learn more about this project, visit ROW at www.row.org.

Get Busy

When we think big for the Lord, it does not necessarily have to involve large numbers of people. Rivers of the World (ROW) is thinking big this month in the Congo and in Brazil with what we call microeconomic projects. In Kenya ROW helped a man buy two chickens, which enabled him to start an egg business. Another microeconomic project is taking a sewing machine to the middle of the Congo and teaching people how to sew and how to turn that skill into a job that provides school uniforms for children.

Penny and her team are heading to Fortaleza, Brazil where they will be working in rural areas helping farmers get just a few more implements for farming the land to increase the yield of their crops. We might not be influencing huge numbers of people but the folks who are being touched are having their lives changed forever. These people will then turn around and influence someone else's life for Jesus Christ.

As you start your day today, may I encourage you to make Psalm 90:17 your prayer? It states:

"May the favor of the Lord our God rest upon us; establish the work of our hands for us—yes, establish the work of our hands."

As a Christian, we should have the desire for all that we do to be reflective of the One who lives within us. Allow Christ to permeate your life so much that whether your job is sweeping floors, inputting data into a computer, operating a business, bagging groceries or supervising a team for a huge corporation, it all counts for Christ.

He Is Our Provider

God provides. Stop a moment to ponder that statement. I can testify to the fact that God provides a way, the means, a friend, a helper, salvation and hope. Let me give you an example that I experienced recently.

I had all of my plans put together. I boarded a plane in Atlanta and flew to Managua, Nicaragua, located near the Pacific Ocean. When I landed, I boarded another plane and flew east to Bluefields, the chief Caribbean port of Nicaragua. I had reserved a car in Bluefields and I had my confirmation number from a major rental car dealership. You can imagine my amazement when I stepped off the plane, tried to find the car I had rented and somebody immediately said, "There's no car rental place here. We're too little."

This was one of those times I was reminded that God provides. Wiley Brown raised his hand and said, "I am your rental car and I am going to get you wherever you need to go, whether that is by planes, trains or automobiles, or even boats." Wiley set us up with taxis and found us a boat during our stay and we were able to complete the job for which we traveled all the way to Nicaragua to do.

As Christians sometimes when people in need cross our paths, we are too quick to say, "Oh, I am so sorry. I'll pray for you. Hope you have a better day." First off, if we tell someone we will pray for them, then that is the time that we should stop everything and pray. Secondly, if someone has a genuine need, then we must do all we can to meet that need because God doesn't give us those opportunities for us to simply say, "I'll pray for you." God expects us to use the resources He has given us to meet the need.

We are reminded of this in James 2:15-16, which says:

"Suppose a brother or sister is without clothes and daily food. If one of you says to him, 'Go, I wish you well; keep warm and well fed,' but does nothing about his physical needs, what good is it?"

His Word Is Powerful

While there is nothing like putting a Bible in somebody's hands, I love using technology to reach people from all over the world. By now, most of you are familiar with the solar powered, digital Bibles that Rivers of the World (ROW) distributes in the various countries that we serve.

We are in the process of using these powerful tools to welcome some folks to Central America, a group of people with a different language, culture and a sometimes very aggressive faith. We used the MegaVoice technology to translate the Word of God into one of their Middle Eastern languages.

Our intention is to encourage Christians in the Monkey Point area of Nicaragua to welcome these visitors from Iran with God's Word and the love of Jesus Christ. Our brothers and sisters in Christ will distribute these audio players to Iranians as they arrive in Nicaragua and will use these devices as a way to introduce the visitors to Jesus and the faith of the folks in the area. The land around Monkey Point has been the home of the Creole folks in the area for generations. By understanding the faith of the folks at Monkey Point, it is our hope that the visitors from Iran and the government of Nicaragua will respect the rights of the indigenous peoples and their land ownership issues.

Will you join with me in prayer that the Lord empowers the people of Monkey Point with boldness and courage to minister to these visitors from Iran? Pray too that once they hear the Word of God in their own language that their hearts and lives will be transformed. We are so grateful that technology can be used to share the Good News of Jesus across the barriers of language, cultures and differing faiths!

We are assured in Hebrews 4:12 (Amplified):

"For the Word that God speaks is alive and full of power [making it active, operative, energizing, and effective]; it is sharper than any two-edged sword, penetrating to the dividing line of the breath of life (soul) and [the immortal] spirit, and of joints and marrow [of the deepest parts of our nature], exposing and sifting and analyzing and judging the very thoughts and purposes of the heart."

Honor Your Elders

Do you cherish the folks in your life who are older? Quite honestly, I enjoy being the old man of our organization, Rivers of the World (ROW). My young staff gets a lot of enjoyment out of making fun of me. I know they really care about me, even when they refer to me as the "old man" or tease me by saying, "Oh, he probably can't do that anymore." They get a big kick out finding out just how much I can still do, even at my age!

Today, I want to cherish a friend of mine who is older than I am, Lt. Gen. Sam Wilson (Ret). I am sure you have heard me speak about Sam from Virginia. He was part of the 5307th Composite Unit (Provisional), popularly known as Merrill's Marauders, in the China-Burma-India Theater during World War II. He is what we call the gray beard—one of the men who really led the way for our country through so many years. In fact, he served under 10 different American presidents.

My friend Sam is just getting over a little heart surgery and they are finding that his heart is as strong as an ox, just like he is. Nonetheless, Sam, get well my friend. Do you have older friends or family whom you are in contact with regularly? Let me encourage you to cherish them for their vast wisdom, which comes from their life's experiences. Spend time listening to them today and above all else, don't ever forget to show them respect.

I bet you didn't realize that God even tells us we are to respect our elders. It's true! Look at Leviticus 19:32 (NKJV):

"'You shall rise before the gray headed and honor the presence of an old man, and fear your God: I *am* the LORD.'"

Joint Heirs

Do you know what Vietnam, Nicaragua, Belize, Congo and Brazil all have in common? During March 2008, Rivers of the World (ROW) had teams stationed in each of those countries sharing the love of God in Jesus Christ. They were in central Vietnam, Belize and Congo and in eastern Brazil and Nicaragua. Regardless of where the teams were, their message of Jesus Christ was the same.

These folks went all over the world, literally, sharing the gospel of hope, peace, truth and joy that is only found in Jesus. Whether it is visiting an orphanage in Vietnam, presenting MegaVoice digital Bibles in Nicaragua or interacting with students at a school in Belize, demonstrating the love of Christ can be conveyed with words or actions. We can tell the people we're visiting that God loves them and that He desires to bless them so they can be a blessing to others.

Today, you may not be in Vietnam, Belize or Brazil, but wherever you are, I want you to realize that God put you there for a reason and that is to share the gospel with someone you meet today. You don't need to use eloquent words to share the love of Christ. It is as simple as giving a stranded mother and her children a ride, saying a kind word to your coworker who is struggling at work or buying a meal for someone who is homeless.

As Christians, we should never forget the privilege we have been given by Christ as joint heirs with the children of Israel for the promise of eternity. We can carry this promise to others overseas or in our neighborhood. Paul tells us in Ephesians 3:6:

"This mystery is that through the gospel the Gentiles are heirs together with Israel, members together of one body, and sharers together in the promise in Christ Jesus."

The greatest gift you can give a person today is the knowledge that no matter what they have done in the past they can be set free in Christ.

Love of Christ

It has been two weeks since Rivers of the World (ROW) has heard from our Kenya program director, Zablon Kuria and our friend, Win Junku. These men are serving in the Rift Valley and in the Mathari Valley. As you might now, Kenya has been thrust into a time of terrible turmoil and upheaval.

Over 1,000 people have lost their lives in the fighting in Kenya. We have received reports that over 300,000 people have been displaced and over 49,000 people have come through refugee camps in the Nakuru area. Hundreds of homes in the Mathari Valley have been looted and destroyed.

Even though we have recently lost communication from these men in Kenya, we know that we serve an ever-present God who is mindful of all things. God knows their struggles, the dangers that exist in that area and the recent chaos that has left so many people without hope.

Christians in America haven't yet experienced real persecution for their faith. Nonetheless, many of us know what it is like to be ridiculed by others for loving Christ, we have experienced lean times in our lives where all we had was our faith in Christ to rest upon and perhaps some of us have endured danger for proclaiming Christ as our Lord. Whatever it is that you are facing today you can be certain that all Christians experience trials and hardships. We have hope, though, and it is found in Romans 8:35, which says:

"Who shall separate us from the love of Christ? Shall trouble or hardship or persecution or famine or nakedness or danger or sword?"

Take heart today, for no matter what you go through, Christ is, and always will be, right by your side!

Mighty Is He

Here is your assignment for today…think big for the Lord. Too often we think in little terms and we pitifully tell God there is no way He could possibly use us because we are too young, old, inexperienced, uneducated, etc.

Springtime has sprung here in the South with grass turning green, flowers blooming, trees, and shrubs coming to life. I have decided to think big this spring by doubling the size of my blueberry plantation here in Georgia. The blueberry bushes will be a wonderful way for me to witness for the Lord because my neighbors will be able to stop by and feed freely on my beautiful, organic Benny's blueberries.

Yes, I am thinking big and I have already made the decision. In fact, today, 3, Rivers of the World's (ROW) executive administrator, is coming over and she is going to help me dig the hole so I can double the size of my plantation from…two blueberry plants to four! I know that may not sound like much, but it sure is to me considering I don't look after the two plants I have and I likely won't look after these two new plants but the Lord will! Before you know it, we will be blessed with lots of blueberries!

Stop for a moment today and think about ways you can influence the world for Jesus in a unique and big way. Don't even think about coming up with reasons why God can't use you. If He can use Gideon, a farmer, to deliver Israel from Midian; David, the shepherd boy and the youngest in his family, to strike down Goliath then go on to be Israel's greatest king; and Mary, a peasant girl, to be the mother of Christ, then He can use you.

If these examples are not enough to convince you, read Exodus chapters 3 and 4. God calls Moses to lead His people out of Egypt. Even though God assures Moses that He will be with him and even performs miracles before

Moses' eyes, Moses, like many of us, still tries to come up with many excuses why he can't possibly be used by God. In Exodus 4:10-12 we read:

"Moses said to the LORD, 'O Lord, I have never been eloquent, neither in the past nor since you have spoken to your servant. I am slow of speech and tongue.' The LORD said to him, 'Who gave man his mouth? Who makes him deaf or mute? Who gives him sight or makes him blind? Is it not I, the LORD? Now go; I will help you speak and will teach you what to say.'"

Do you think Moses was finally obedient? No, he continued to protest that God use someone else. Instead, God used Aaron to be the mouthpiece for Moses, all the while still using Moses to complete His plan. Quit making excuses today and recognize that God's power is within you.

Mistakes

Are you like many people when you make a mistake you beat yourself up? Let me tell you about a little mistake I made the other day. I had just arrived back in the States from being out in the jungle and I had brought back with me a fungus growing on my feet.

To eliminate the fungus I have to apply this goo directly on my feet. This sounds easy enough, huh? Well, one night before I went to bed I didn't have my glasses on and I applied what I thought was the goo for the fungus. I woke up the next morning to realize I did put something like goo on my feet, but it actually was toothpaste! My feet smelled minty fresh but I still had the fungus on my feet!

I had two choices—I could have gotten upset at myself or I could have simply laughed at my mistake. I decided that I would do the best that I can, when I can and if I fall short, I will cut myself some slack.

Are you struggling today with some mistakes that you have made? Some folks spend years, and even a lifetime full of regret and guilt for past mistakes. Guilt can be a good tool to lead us to our knees in repentance, asking Jesus for forgiveness. However, we must then accept His gracious forgiveness and move on. If you are having a difficult time releasing your past mistakes, ask yourself this question, "If Christ can forgive me of my sins, then who am I to not forgive myself of my mistakes?"

There are times in our lives that we knowingly sin, but there are also those times that we are unaware of some sin that we may have committed. Make it a habit each day to ask Christ to forgive you of your sins—the ones you are aware of and those you are not. May your prayer today be Psalm 19:12-13, which says:

"Who can discern his errors? Forgive my hidden faults. Keep your servant also from willful sins; may they not rule over me. Then will I be blameless, innocent of great transgression."

Would you like to make a difference in the lives of others by sharing the new life Christ has given you? Visit the Rivers of the World (ROW) web site, www.row.org, to see how you can share the Gospel of Christ with the world.

New Start

Within the first week of this new year, I will be in four different countries. It is hard to imagine but during that first week, I will visit two countries in the Middle East, I will arrive home to a country that I call home, the United States, and then I will pack my things and head to the exciting work of Rivers of the World (ROW) in the Dominican Republic.

The crew traveling to the Dominican Republic will consist of me, my son Adam, a team from Hampden-Sydney College and the Dean of Students from the college, along with his wife and three daughters. Our goal is to build latrines, conduct vacation Bible school and share the love of Christ with people who risked everything to cross the mountains of Haiti into the Dominican Republic with the hope of starting a new life.

Our work in the Dominican Republic is centered in the bateys, which is a name for the poor villages where Haitian refugees reside on sugar cane plantations. Can you imagine beginning the new year by lending a hand to make life more bearable for people who are starting a brand new life in the wonderful and beautiful Dominican Republic?

These Haitian refugees risked their lives for a chance at a better life in the Dominican Republic. For those folks who are living life without Christ, all they have to do is ask for forgiveness, repent of their sins and take a step of faith by accepting Jesus as their Savior. That simple, yet priceless act, allows individuals to experience a brand new life in Christ. We are promised in 2 Corinthians 5:17 (Amplified):

"Therefore if any person is [ingrafted] in Christ (the Messiah) he is a new creation (a new creature altogether); the old [previous moral and spiritual condition] has passed away. Behold, the fresh and new has come!"

If you are searching for new ways that you can serve the Lord, check us out at www.row.org.

Night Is Coming

I just returned from a trip to the Dominican Republic, where I served alongside some young college students from Hampden-Sydney College, located in Hampden-Sydney, Va. My young college friends have to be exhausted.

We had an intriguing week in the Dominican Republic working what is called batay seven. This is a refugee camp for Haitian folks who have come over the mountains looking for a better way of life. We had an opportunity to help make their lives a bit easier.

Hampden-Sydney College, a private men's college, sends teams to serve with Rivers of the World (ROW) and usually this includes a very strong bunch of young men. On this trip, we also had the Dean of Students Dr. David A. Klein, his wife and his three daughters. The young men all behaved a little better. Everyone was a little more polite and we worked harder trying to impress D.A., his wife and his three daughters.

The exciting part about this recent trip was that we managed to put 10 latrines into the village. This simple and practical task will allow the people to get rid of a third of their disease in that community. It comes back to the same old point, "It's not hard to change the world, you just have to do it."

It is easy to feel overwhelmed when you consider the vast need of people worldwide. Instead of not even trying to do your part, may I remind you what John 9:4 says:

"As long as it is day, we must do the work of him who sent me. Night is coming, when no one can work."

No effort is too small in the Kingdom of God. If you are able to do manual work, then find a ministry and work with all your might. If you have been blessed with the skill of organizing and delegating, then use that gift to meet the needs of others. The greatest and most powerful thing we can do to minister to others is often overlooked—prayer.

If you are unable to serve with ROW, then let me encourage you to pray for all those who serve ROW around the world. Visit us at www.row.org.

One Lord

One of the highlights of my travels is visiting with folks across our radio listening audience. I recently had so much fun visiting two churches in Omaha, Neb. Several of the men took me hunting and we just had the best time! They took a Georgia boy out in nine-degree weather and about a foot of snow! It was incredible.

After my hunting excursion, I attended a men's dinner. People came from all around Omaha. We ate some of the best venison and elk—the best I had all day long! The greatest part about visiting with our radio listeners is we all have one thing in common—our love for the Lord. This gives us a foundation for friendships that just can't be beat.

Regardless of our denomination, if we have accepted Christ as our Lord and Savior, then we are all part of one body of believers. Paul tells us in Ephesians 4:4-6 (Amplified):

"[There is] one body and one Spirit—just as there is also one hope [that belongs] to the calling you received—[There is] one Lord, one faith, one baptism, One God and Father of [us] all, Who is above all [Sovereign over all], pervading all and [living] in [us] all."

It is great to fellowship and worship in our home church, but let me encourage you to take time this week to also fellowship with other Christians. Go out to lunch and spend time talking about how good the Lord has been In your life. Attend a Christian concert and unite together in worshipping Jesus. Above all else, take time to encourage and build up those in your church and those serving the Lord elsewhere.

Preparing the Way

Rivers of the World (ROW) has recently taken some steps to ensure the gospel of Jesus Christ goes forth in Nicaragua, even to visitors from Iran. There is no way to describe how surprised the people of Monkey Point, Nicaragua were when Revolutionary Guard troops from Iran stepped off helicopters and into their village in November 2007.

The goal by Iran is to construct a dry canal across Nicaragua and to create a deep-water port near Monkey Point. After hearing of the visit by the Iranian soldiers to Monkey Point, Dr. Chris Price, senior minister of St. Luke's Presbyterian Church in Dunwoody, Ga., and I scheduled a trip to meet with village leaders.

In preparation for the soldiers return, we wanted to equip the people of Monkey Point with Bibles in order to share Jesus with these visitors. We have supplied village leaders in Monkey Point with digital solar powered Bibles in English and others translated into Spanish and Farsi, the native language of Iran. ROW has also added a new roof to the church in Monkey Point, renovated their school and even sent baseball equipment to the village.

Despite how surprised the people of Monkey Point were by the Iranian soldiers, they didn't shrink in fear, but instead, they courageously sought ways to share Christ with the visitors. Paul gave Timothy the charge in 2 Timothy 4:2:

"Preach the Word; be prepared in season and out of season; correct, rebuke and encourage—with great patience and careful instruction."

As followers of Christ, we must take advantage of every opportunity the Lord provides us in sharing the life-saving Gospel with others. It is imperative to hide the Word of God in our hearts so that we may be prepared in and out of season.

Removing Obstacles

One of the favorite television shows of folks here at Rivers of the World (ROW) is "Everybody Loves Raymond," featuring lead characters Raymond Romano and two-time Emmy award winner Patricia Heaton. Ms. Heaton recently did a wonderful thing in support of ROW.

One of the chapters of ROW is called ROW Kids, which focuses its efforts on children all over the world, whether it is providing food, clothing or education. Ms. Heaton was kind enough to do a video on You Tube on behalf of ROW, specifically promoting ROW Kids. On the video, Ms. Heaton describes a girl in Belize who had to drop out of school at age 12. Shortly after ROW Kids was established, this girl was provided a scholarship and later obtained a job working at a large resort.

In July 2005, participants of a church-sponsored mission trip to Billy White, Belize saw firsthand that poverty in this small rural town was the result of the limited educational opportunities for the children in Billy White. Following that mission trip, ROW Kids was created and has since grown from the small village of Billy White to examining the needs of children in six countries, over four continents. One of the main goals of ROW Kids is to break the cycle of poverty and economic exploitation through the improvement of children's educational opportunities.

Educational programs administered by ROW Kids focus on removing obstacles to school attendance and performance and providing each child a means to obtain the necessary education to bring them out of their dire poverty. These children need the basic necessities, such as clothing, shoes, books, paper and educational materials in order to achieve an education.

As Christians, we should strive to do our part to remove any obstacles that may be standing in the way of any child receiving an education, which would allow them to become productive citizens in society. We are given a command in Deuteronomy 15:11, which says:

"There will always be poor people in the land. Therefore I command you to be openhanded toward your brothers and toward the poor and needy in your land."

If you are interested in ways you can help provide an education to children through ROW Kids, visit us at www.rowkids.org.

Rescue the Weak

Chickens, pigs and goats, pots, pans and plants. Let's say that again…chickens, pigs and goats, pots, pans and plants. Unbelievably, these are the things that Rivers of the World (ROW) has been asked for by the people of the Mathari Valley who have lost so much in the recent fighting in Kenya.

None of the items these people are requesting is that expensive. It cost around $50 for a good goat and about $20 for pots and pans. Can you assist ROW in helping us to meet the basic needs of the people of the Mathari Valley?

One of the goals for ROW is to equip these families with small microeconomic opportunities. This would include raising chickens, pigs and goats as well as using pots, pans and plants to supplement their lives.

As Christians, we are instructed in Psalm 82:3-4:

"Defend the cause of the weak and fatherless; maintain the rights of the poor and oppressed. Rescue the weak and needy; deliver them from the hand of the wicked."

The people of the Mathari Valley have undergone extreme persecution, which has resulted in the loss of material possessions, homes and even lives in Kenya. It is up to God to bring about reconciliation in that country, but it is up to us to meet the needs of those who have been displaced.

Serving the Yagua Indians

Let me tell you a little bit about my dad, who is affectionately called, "paw, paw." My dad, Dr. Gordon Mathes, has reached that age where he can wear plaids and stripes and get away with it. It doesn't matter if his clothes match or not, just as long as he likes it, then he can wear it.

Now let me tell you about another "match" that is far more important. Rivers of the World (ROW) has recently received a matching grant for the construction of a hospital ship in Peru. The boat will be built and based in Iquitos, Peru. We have a partnership with Project Amazonas, the University of Mississippi Medical School and the Loreto Region Ministry of Health. Each group will work to keep the boat serving the Yagua Indians, the indigenous people who gave the Amazon River its name.

We have the potential to obtain $100,000 toward this project. For every dollar we raise, it will be matched up to $50,000. Once built, the ship will serve along the Amazon, Napo, Nanay, Oroso, Galves, Yavari, Apayacu and the Anayacu rivers. We will have the ability to help the Yagua meet their educational, health, water and evangelistic needs.

Would you take a moment today and pray that ROW is able to match this generous grant? While you're praying, ask the Lord how you can help, whether it is simply praying each day, volunteering to serve with ROW or donating a portion of what the Lord has blessed you with in order to meet the needs of the Yagua Indians.

Speaking to the 12 disciples, Jesus instructed them to go to the "lost sheep of Israel." In Matthew 10:8, we read that as the disciples went they were to preach the message:

"Heal the sick, raise the dead, cleanse those who have leprosy, drive out demons. Freely you have received, freely give."

As followers of Christ, we too have been given authority to drive out evil spirits and to heal every disease and sickness. The construction of this ship in Peru will enable ROW to combine modern medicine with the healing power of prayer to minister to those in need.

Simple Plan, Daily Walk

Many of you know the name of Rivers of the World's (ROW) administrator because actually, it is not really a name at all. She goes by 3. She signs her name 3, her business cards have 3 on it and even her stationary has her name, the number 3 on it. If you ever get the chance to meet her, take a close look at her clothing because somewhere you will find her name, 3, monogrammed.

3 is about to be in a production of "Sleeping Beauty," where she will be able to display one of her many talents. She is a ballerina. I have the honor of attending the show. I am just going to sit there and be amazed that the cast can perform so many difficult maneuvers all the while making it look effortless.

When you think about it, serving the Lord is the same way. Whether you are in America or anywhere else in the world, serving the Lord can appear very complicated and difficult. However, just like ballet, the more you practice the more it becomes second nature. You have a bad thought and you instantly ask the Lord to purify your thoughts. You say something without thinking and offend someone, the Holy Spirit quickens you, and immediately you repent and ask for forgiveness.

Too many times people lose sight of how easy it is to accept salvation and how straightforward it is to maintain their walk with the Lord. We don't need to clean ourselves up, change our lives or perform a set number of good deeds to be saved. The simple plan is detailed in Romans 10:9, which says:

"That if you confess with your mouth, 'Jesus is Lord,' and believe in your heart that God raised him from the dead, you will be saved."

Don't make it more complicated then it is. Simply believe in your heart that Christ died for your sins, rose again on the third day, confess to Him your sins, ask for forgiveness and you will receive the glorious gift of salvation.

Once you become a Christian, walking with the Lord daily is just as uncomplicated. We learn in Luke 9:23:

"Then he said to them all: 'If anyone would come after me, he must deny himself and take up his cross daily and follow me.'"

There are three things we must do to daily walk with Jesus. We must put aside our selfish desires, align our hearts and mind with Christ daily and follow Him. Simply put, we must daily strive to imitate Christ in every aspect of our lives.

Singing For the Children

It just thrills my soul when people from around the world come together to help other folks in the world for the sake of Jesus Christ. Check your calendar...do you have anything planned March 28 or 29? If not, head to Belize where you can take part in a benefit concert to help the children of Belize attain better education opportunities.

Rhythm of Chance, located in Belize, and ROW Kids will hold joint concerts, one in Belize City on March 29, 2008 and the other in San Ignacio on March 28, 2008. The ROC & ROW Kids for Education benefit concert is being held to raise funds to assist with the educational needs of underprivileged children in Belize. Featured during the concerts will be Christian rock artists Everlife, from Nashville and Chasen from South Carolina.

These concerts are a great way for the young people of Belize to hear about Christ through music. It is also a wonderful opportunity for Rivers of the World (ROW) to assist the children of the Billy White area, where we have a school. We want to do more than house, feed and educate these children. We want to help them either finish a trade school or obtain a university education, which will equip them with the skills they need to be productive citizens in their country.

Delivering the message of Christ to the world can be done through preaching His Word, praying with others, serving those in need and even by worshipping Him in music. We discover in Psalm 92:1-3 that music is an integral part of expressing our gratitude to God for all His many blessings:

"It is good to praise the LORD and make music to your name, O Most High, to proclaim your love in the morning and your faithfulness at night, to the music of the ten-stringed lyre and the melody of the harp."

Whether it is with a flute, electric guitar, drums, piano or simply our voices, let us never forget to worship the Lord. Sing, play music or even dance this day to show Jesus how much you Love Him because of His goodness, His love and His mercy.

Stay Connected

Oh, you will get a kick out of this! I just looked at my calendar and I realized that during the next two weeks I have appointments to see three different physicians. As if that isn't enough, I also have an appointment with a dentist.

Yes, it is that time again for me to get checkups and to get things straightened out and fixed that have either been broken or worn out through so many years of working in jungles. These checkups for my physical body make me wonder if we, as Christians, ever sit down and do spiritual checkups.

When was the last time you sat down with your pastor or a trusted Christian friend and asked that they examine your life? It would be good to ask them to offer insight into the areas of your life where you are strong spiritually. Similarly, you should also ask that they reveal to you areas of weaknesses. It is these areas that you and your pastor or close Christian friend can offer up to the Lord in prayer.

Pause for a few moments today and ask yourself, "Am I stronger spiritually today compared to this time last year? Do the same sins and shortcomings trip me up that have plagued me for years? Am I honestly growing in the Lord or have I become stagnant in my walk with Jesus?"

Jesus warns us clearly in John 15:1-2:

"I am the true vine, and my Father is the gardener. He cuts off every branch in me that bears no fruit, while every branch that does bear fruit he prunes so that it will be even more fruitful."

To avoid being cut off from the life giving power of the Lord, let me encourage you to set aside time regularly to conduct spiritual checkups of your life. There is no middle ground in our walk with the Lord. Either we are growing spiritually or we are not.

Thank You

Oh, my, this could be the "big one!" I live in Dixie, more specifically Georgia, and it just started to snow. When it snows even just a little bit in the South people make a mad dash to the hardware store and buy everything they ever dreamed of buying. People also rush to the grocery store to stock up on staple items, as I did. I just bought 18 loaves of bread, three gallons of milk, four gallons of water and enough toilet paper to wrap the whole neighborhood. I am now prepared and just waiting for the snow to pile up in case this is the "big one."

Isn't it funny the way we respond to things? Let me ask you today, how do you respond to blessings in your life, not adversities, but blessings? When the Lord does something good for you, do you just say thank you Lord and charge ahead or do you wonder what is going to happen next?

When you receive a promotion at work, do you pat yourself on the back and get prideful thinking you deserved the promotion based upon your outstanding abilities? When you are appointed to be in charge of something at church do you automatically assume it was because of your wonderful talents? We must realize that all good things come from the Lord. We are nothing apart from God.

The next time you are inclined to take credit for anything good that comes your way, read Psalm 44:8, which says:

"In God we make our boast all day long, and we will praise your name forever. Selah."

We should not only thank the Lord for all our many blessings each day, but we should also simply thank Him for His love, grace, mercy and forgiveness.

To the Ends of the Earth

Do you have a few moments for us to do a quick survey? Rivers of the World (ROW) has just purchased satellite equipment that will enable us to do a live broadcast from very remote jungles around the world. We could broadcast live over the Internet through a video conferencing site.

There is no cost for people who view the site…all you would have to do is register, sign on and watch a live broadcast of ROW. What I would like to know, before ROW further invests in this project, is whether or not anybody would be interested in watching live broadcasts of ROW.

Everyone is familiar with the various reality TV shows that are currently aired. With this technology, you can watch as we travel the Congo River or visit the orphanage in Kinshasa in the Congo. You will have the opportunity to watch ROW teams as they serve along the Napo, Oroso, Yanayaku and the Apayaku rivers in Peru. In other segments, you can watch ROW live as we travel to Vietnam, Honduras, Belize and other countries we serve. Are you interested in watching a broadcast live over the Internet of all the ways ROW serves others around the world? If so, contact me at ben@row.org.

May I remind you as Christians it is the responsibility of each of us to deliver the good news of Jesus Christ to the ends of the earth? For some of us, that might mean simply witnessing in our neighborhood, town or state. However, for others, like us at ROW, it means literally traveling to remote areas and being the hands, feet, voice and heart of Jesus.

Jesus tells us in Acts 13:47 (Amplified):

"For so the Lord has charged us, saying, I have set you to be a light for the Gentiles (the heathen), that you may bring [eternal] salvation to the uttermost parts of the earth."

To Win Many

No matter how often I hear people say, "do you know I think the Lord is calling me to ministry," I never grow tired of it. I just finished being a keynote speaker at a mission's conference here in Georgia. After the conference, my new friend, Mark, came up to me and said, "We've got to go eat lunch and we've got to do it right now."

Well you know me, I am not going to get in the way of a good meal or the Lord! We got in Mark's car and headed to Rudolph's Restaurant for lunch. He looked across the table at me and said, "God has called me to ministry." Mark is a businessman! I replied, "Tell me what the Lord has told you."

My friend, Mark, said he is committed to starting an organization that will put roofs up first as we build new churches. Well do I have news for him! Rivers of the World (ROW) needs to build around 80 churches in Brazil and at least that many in Honduras. These projects start now and it is all because one man said, "I believe the Lord has called me to serve."

How about you? Has the Lord called you to serve in some capacity? There are those folks who are called by God to be pastors, teachers and evangelists, but all of us who are Christians are called into ministry. We need a humble spirit and a servant's heart like the Apostle Paul who said in 1 Corinthians 9:19:

"Though I am free and belong to no man, I make myself a slave to everyone, to win as many as possible."

What can you do today to win lost souls for Jesus Christ?

Unchanging Lord

If you make your living by traveling often then you can count on a few things that are always constant. You can be certain there will be traffic, road construction and there will always be somebody who decides they are going to have a wreck the day you're trying to get somewhere important. The other thing you can count on during your travels is seeing friends.

Within the last five days, I have been at First Presbyterian Church in Meridian, Miss., up in the mountains of east Tennessee with folks from First Baptist Church of Dalton, Ga., spoke at a meeting at Georgia Tech in Atlanta and ended my weekend at Covenant Presbyterian Church down in Albany, Ga., located in the southwest corner of the state.

During my travels over the last five days, I encountered those constants. There were wrecks, traffic and lousy weather. The other constant was also prevalent. In each location there were wonderful, precious friends whom I have spent my life with for the last 30 years. We shared our love for the Lord, for this world and for changing the world for Christ.

If your faith is wavering today and you are wondering where God is in your life, let me encourage you to commit to memory Hebrews 13:8, which says:

"Jesus Christ is the same yesterday and today and forever."

This means the same God who healed your body last year and the same God who allowed you to wake up this morning is the same God who will provide all that you have need of forevermore. This includes friendship, comfort, encouragement, strength, sound mind and joy beyond measure.

Useful For Life

Have you discovered that business negotiations can be rather tricky? My friends at Monkey Point, Nicaragua are doing something unique in handling a complicated situation.

Representatives from Iran have recently landed at Monkey Point with the intention of installing a canal that would stretch all the way across Nicaragua. Since the proposed canal would begin at Monkey Point, the citizens have begun to prepare for business negotiations. They have equipped themselves with solar powered digital Bibles with Scripture that has been translated into Farsi, the language of the people of Iran.

The citizens intend on meeting with the Iranian leaders and telling them, "Before we discuss jobs, land ownership and faith, we would like for you to listen to the Word of God. We can then get back together and visit." That is a wonderful approach to business dealings. Can you imagine reading Scripture before a company business meeting? How about reading God's word and praying before conducting business with your partner?

Hearing the Word of God preached during Sunday morning services is not sufficient to sustain a person in their walk as a Christian. We read in 2 Timothy 3:16-17:

"All Scripture is God-breathed and is useful for teaching, rebuking, correcting and training in righteousness, so that the man of God may be thoroughly equipped for every good work."

We must understand that Scripture is intended to be our daily nourishment for every aspect of our lives. If you desire a healing touch, wisdom, victory over sin, direction, comfort, friendship or to know Jesus more, then delve into Scripture.

Welcome Home

There are some things that you just wonder about. For instance, I have often wondered what it is like for a military family when their loved one returns from fighting in Iraq or Afghanistan after being gone for a long time. I can relate from the perspective of a father because my son just returned from Iraq and that was very exciting.

I will soon be experiencing another reunion in about two weeks when my wife, Mickie, returns to the United States after having served as a college professor at the University of Qatar in Doha since August 2007.

While Mickie has been gone, I have been learning how to cook, clean, pay all the bills and look after the house. Now all of a sudden she is going to be busting in here expecting to take things over even though she will only be home for five days.

Will you join with me today in praying for all of us who deal with folks who come and go in our lives, whether it is because of a career or military commitment? We need to determine the best way to except our family and friends and welcome them home with an open spirit of love, grace and mercy.

As Christians, our salvation is founded upon faith, but then must be rooted in faithful service to our Lord. We are not saved by our good works and deeds, however, once we accept Christ as our Savior, we should naturally feel compelled to follow in the footsteps of our Master. Peter instructs us in 2 Peter 1:10-11:

"Therefore, my brothers, be all the more eager to make your calling and election sure. For if you do these things, you will never fall, and you will receive a rich welcome into the eternal kingdom of our Lord and Savior Jesus Christ."

Let us strive each day to give our all for the One who gave His all for us. Just imagine that day when He calls us home and welcomes us with open arms and with the loving words, "Well done my good and faithful servant."